To A Very Special Boy:

All BOYS love Easter
bunnies, chocolate, egg games,
and a basket full of goodies!

I hope Easter is egg~citing...
filled with fun and adventure
for a SPECIAL BOY!

A BOY as special as you
should get your favorite
treats from the Easter bunny!

Here's wishing a SPECIAL BOY
an EGG-STRA special Easter!

HOP! HOP! HOP! The Easter Bunny is on its way to make sure you have plenty of sweet treats!

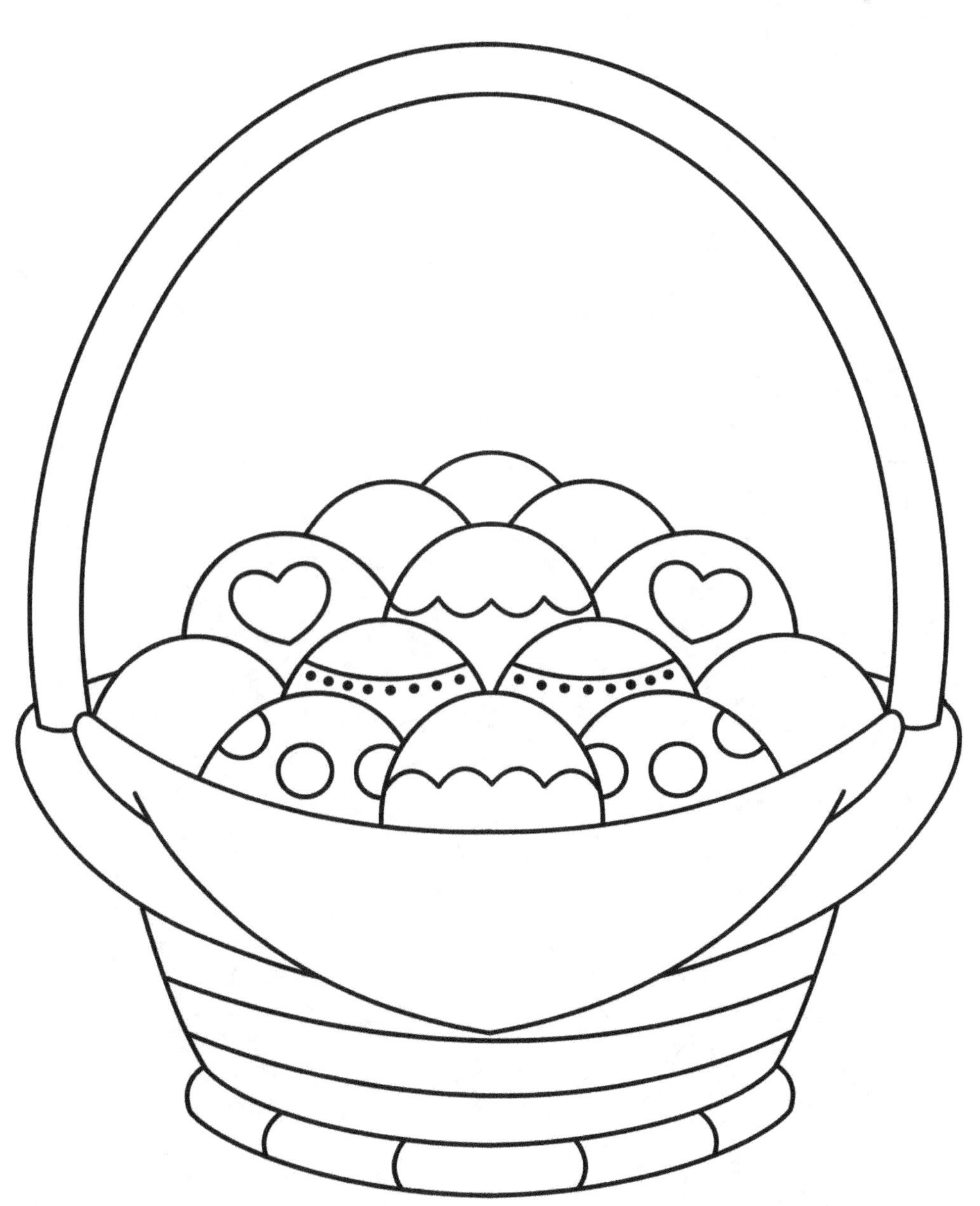

Wishing you a wonderful time as you celebrate Easter with family & friends!

One of the best things about Easter is...
all of the chocolate eggs
SPECIAL BOYS get to eat!

The Easter Bunny told me that you are an EGG-STRA SPECIAL BOY!

I hope that you have an
EGG-CELLENT
Easter this year!

Have a very Hoppy Easter!

I hope you have the best luck this year on your Easter egg hunt!

To A Special Boy from the
Easter Bunny!
(Coloring Card)
(Personalized Card) Easter Messages,
Greetings, Poems for Children!

HAPPY EASTER!
TO A VERY SPECIAL BOY
FROM THE EASTER BUNNY!